Death of the Elephant

VOLUME ONE OF BARSIDE CHATS WITH AMERICA

GIL GROSSI

PAGE PUBLISHING
Conneaut Lake, PA

First originally published by Page Publishing 2021

ISBN 978-1-6624-5430-1 (pbk)
ISBN 978-1-6624-5431-8 (digital)

Printed in the United States of America

INTRODUCTION

Just by way of introduction, I'm Gil Grossi. I'm not a politician; never been elected to any office. I'm not a member of the media or a pundit from TV. I'm just a seventy-year-old guy who has never seen anything close to what has been going on in this country for the past four years. And who sees our two-party political system in the greatest jeopardy that it has ever been in our history. In order to support what I'm about to say in the pages that follow, I must reveal that I do have a BA in political science from the University of Illinois. I was a prosecutor for eleven years, an associate judge for twenty-three years (appointed position), and a law school professor for twenty-seven years. When I taught law students how to try cases, I always gave them the following advice—talk to the jurors just as you would if you were having a drink with them at a bar (minus the swearing). I intend to follow my own advice and write this book in exactly the same way. So pour yourself your favorite drink, alcoholic or not, and let's have at it.

PROLOGUE

Cartoonist Thomas Nash is credited with giving the Democratic Party the symbol of a donkey and in 1874 the Republican Party the symbol of the elephant. I'm quite sure that he never imagined that they would last all the way until 2020. The question that I have is just how much longer the Republican Party and its symbol can continue to exist. My firm belief is that if Donald Trump had not won the election of 2016, there would never have been another Republican president in this country. Donald Trump's election in 2016 galvanized the Republican base in a way that no other candidate could have. That same thing happened again in 2020, with Trump getting 10 million more votes than he did in 2016. However, Donald Trump was a generational phenomenon. Without him at the helm for the next four years, the future of the Republican Party seems to be hanging in the balance. This reminds me of the scene in Charles Dickens' *A Christmas Carol,* when the Ghost of

Christmas Future shows Ebenezer Scrooge his own grave. Ebenezer asks the Ghost, "Are these the shadows of things that will be or may be, only?" For our purposes, is the death of the Republican Party inevitable or can events change it? That's what we will be exploring in this book.

CHAPTER 1

Storm Clouds on the Horizon

There are several initial issues that cannot be ignored. First, in an analysis from the University of Virginia released in July 2018, it was determined that there are twelve million more registered Democrats than Republicans nationwide. At first glance, this number sounds scary for the Republicans. Upon closer examination, however, it's not quite as bad. Only thirty-one of the fifty states register voters by party. This means that we don't know what is going on in the remaining nineteen states, some of which were won by Donald Trump in 2016. Additionally, some people don't like to declare their party affiliation, so the margin may be smaller. That being said, twelve million voters is still a large deficit to be dealing with.

Second, the election of 2018 was a serious blow to the Republicans in the House of Representatives. Republicans lost forty seats. While not as disastrous as the sixty-three seats lost in 2010 by the Democrats, losing the House was nonetheless a serious blow to Republicans. What is of even greater concern was the turnout: Democrats 59.4 million; Republicans 50.4 million. This is nine million fewer voters.

Beyond the numbers, the Democrats regaining control of the House has resulted in an avalanche of investigations, which culminated in President Trump's impeachment. The only mitigating factor to all this is that the Republicans did gain two seats in the Senate.

The third initial issue is that changing demographics is turning traditional red states either purple or blue. Policies, like high taxes, in states like New York, California, and Illinois have driven liberal voters out. They have moved to states like Texas, New Hampshire, Arizona, Florida, and Tennessee. This has contributed to the process of turning these states purple or at least, less red. Traditional Republican states like Colorado and Utah are similarly turning purple.

What happened in specific midterm races gives even greater cause for alarm for Republicans. Incumbent Republican Senator Ted Cruz had a very close contest with an unproven, little-known, former Congressman

Beto O'Rourke. In the traditional Republican strongholds of Georgia and Florida, the races for governor resulted in razor-thin wins for the Republicans against candidates that were decidedly leftist liberals with significant baggage. Not to mention, Democrats gaining control of both Houses of the Virginia state legislature.

The election of 2020 provided even more dire news for the Republican Party and its elephant symbol. Arizona, a former Republican stronghold, went Democratic. Wisconsin, Michigan, Pennsylvania, which Trump had won in 2016, went back into the Democratic column. But by far, the worst sign of all was Georgia, a solid red state since 2000. How did this happen in a state with a Republican Secretary of State, a Republican Governor, and both state houses Republican? How did Georgia elect two Socialist, Marxist candidates, with other highly negative baggage, knowing full well that they were giving Democrats control of the Senate?

All these factors provide a backdrop that causes serious concerns for the future of the Republican Party. The totality of these cannot be minimized. They truly reveal that there are storm clouds on the horizon for the future of the Republican Party.

Chapter 2

It's All About the Base

Donald Trump changed the Republican Party in many ways, for the better. His populist approach tapped into feelings of neglect and frustration by the average American working class, who had a distrust of big government. Look at the coalition that Trump put together in 2020, expanding his vote total by ten million over 2016; the working class, more Hispanics and African-Americans than any other Republican in history and older voters. The question is can Republicans hold this base together if Donald Trump is no longer in the picture? Trump was a once-in-a-generation, larger-than-life figure. Will that base now fall apart?

In addition, how can that base be expanded? The answer to these questions will determine the future of the Republican Party.

Meanwhile, look at what the Democrats are doing to both firm up and expand their base. First, they are making a totally transparent appeal to younger voters. Their promises of canceling student loan debt and free college education have visions of sugar plums dancing in the heads of our nation's youth. Talk about trying to buy votes. This is nothing but crass socialism that flies in the face of our free enterprise system. How is that fair to all those people who honored their commitments and paid off their loans? Since when did not honoring a promise or disregarding a contract become a good thing? When it means getting more votes, that's when. Why stop there? Why not cancel all car loans and mortgages too while we're at it?

Second, Democrats are appealing to all those who favor abortion by expanding it to new heights—third term and late-term abortions up to the moment of birth and even after birth.

Third, Democrats are currying favor with those who oppose gun ownership and the Second Amendment right to bear arms. They start small with background checks, then move to banning assault rifles. The next step will be an outright ban on guns and elimination of the Second Amendment altogether.

Fourth, HB1 is trying to give the right to vote to prisoners and convicted felons. These will all go right into the Democratic column.

Finally, the biggest one of all. Under Joe Biden, the Democrats will change immigration law to give fifteen million illegal immigrants the right to vote. Guess which party they will be voting for?

So how can the Republican Party counter this expansion of the Democratic base? Because if it can't, the death of the elephant is a certainty.

CHAPTER 3

Capturing the Youth Vote

Capturing the youth vote will be no easy task for Republicans. How do you counter free stuff?

How do you make them see that short-term gain will lead to long-term pain?

This has to be approached on several levels. First, all federal student loans should be completely forgiven if a person works for the government, on any level, for a specified number of years.

This will also foster public service.

Next, the interest rate on student loans should be extremely low. Then, all repayment periods should be thirty years, not as low as ten as they are now. Second, the costs of college education need to be lowered. There is more control over state-run schools, so that is where they need to start.

Third, the education system in the country needs to be examined and changed. The education system is producing left-wing liberal, socialist students already programmed to accept the progressive, Marxist ideology being currently advocated by the Democratic Party. College campuses have been overrun by socialist, left-leaning professors, who don't tolerate deviation from their ideology. Conservative speakers are banned from speaking on campuses. Students are being taught that America is a systemically racist country, that capitalism is a flawed system, that America is the problem, not the solution; and that we should be ashamed of our history, not proud of it.

This isn't just happening at the college level. The indoctrination is starting in grammar school and high school. Schools across the country are now teaching a history curriculum based on the 1619 Project. This is a series of essays that claims that America was actually founded in 1619, when slavey was first introduced into the country and that it continues to discriminate against Black Americans. This is a sinister and dangerous attempt to rewrite and misrepresent US history in the classrooms and warp the impressionable minds of our children. This is being done for a personal goal—to push leftist ideology and obtain reparations.

Take a look at what is happening around the country right now. A Massachusetts school has banned Homer's

The Odyssey. Teachers are refusing to teach novels by F. Scott Fitzgerald and Dr. Seuss, along with classics such as Nathaniel Hawthorne's *The Scarlet Letter.*

In San Francisco, the school district has proposed changing the names of forty-four schools, banning such names as Washington, Jefferson, and Lincoln instead of focusing on reopening schools, so students can get back into classrooms and learn. This is part of the larger attempt across the country to rewrite our nation's history and cancel anything that disagrees with the left's ideology.

This should serve as a clear warning to parents across the country. Pay close attention to what your children are being taught in school. If you are able, get appointed to local school boards, so you can affect policy. If not, then band together with other parents to force a return to actual American history, warts and all, so that we can learn from the past, not eliminate it. If we lose the battle for the minds and souls of our children, then all else is lost.

CHAPTER 4

Abortion

There is no issue that evokes more emotion than that of abortion. The rallying cry both for and against *Roe v. Wade* can be heard across the land. Those people against abortion believe life begins at birth, based on religious and moral grounds. Those beliefs cannot be shaken.

Those people who support abortion believe it's a woman's right to choose, to control her own body. That belief is equally as strong.

I make no personal comment on one side or the other at the outset. Let's first take a look at the case of *Roe v. Wade.* I'll put on my judge's hat, just once, for this one. Roe was decided by the US Supreme Court in 1973. In a nutshell, the Court held that Texas's attempt to ban abortions was unconstitutional, as a violation of the right to privacy implicit in the 14th Amendment of the US Constitution. This case was one of the greatest, if not the greatest, examples of judicial activism in American jurisprudence. First of all, there is no right to privacy in the Constitution anywhere, despite the Court's previously creating it in another act of judicial activism in the case of *Griswold v. Connecticut.* Second, there is no right to an abortion or to control a woman's body anywhere in the Constitution either. Third, the right to an abortion is not part of the right to privacy either way. This was judicial activism purely and simply.

Now, as I said earlier, I'm not saying that abortion is right or wrong, I'm simply saying that it is not a right protected under the US Constitution. This is an issue that should be left to each state individually. As a practical and legal matter, Roe will never be overruled. However, it needs to be limited and distinguished. Here's how and why.

Even if a woman has a right to control her own body under the US Constitution, that right, like every other right even freedom of speech, is not absolute. It must fall if it comes into conflict with a greater right—the right to life. The Supreme Court was misguided in Roe when it created arbitrary trimesters. The issue should be viability— can the fetus live outside the womb? Viability traditionally has been viewed to be twenty-eight weeks or seven months.

However, science and medicine has advanced to where babies born as early as twenty-three weeks now survive.

Therefore, viability should be the critical tipping point at which the right to control your body must yield to the right to life. Since the Supreme Court is unlikely to overturn Roe, it must then limit abortion to the first twenty-three weeks when viability kicks in and then only allow it after that, if the mother's life is at stake.

Late-term abortion is an area where Republicans can look to expand their base. They need to appeal to Democrats who oppose late-term abortions, and there are plenty of them. The polls on the issue are confusing and can be misleading because they are dependent on how the questions are phrased. Most people oppose overturning Roe outright. However, when the question is phrased, "Do you favor abortion in all or most circumstances?" the percentages in a recent Gallup poll are high: 88 percent of Democrats, 76 percent of Independents, and even 59 percent of Republicans agree. The problem comes in when you specify what circumstances do you not favor abortion. When polled about third-trimester abortion, the numbers in support of abortion plummet. For example, in a series of Gallup polls conducted in July 2018, only 20 percent of people favored third-term abortions. Other Gallup polls in late 2020 have found that between 8–12 percent of Democrats oppose abortion altogether. The point of all this is that there are millions of Democrats out there who can woo away from a Party getting more extreme about abortion every day. The most glaring example of extremism being Governor Northrup of Virginia who suggested that even after birth, the baby could be made comfortable while the mother and doctor decide whether to abort the baby after birth, which amounts to infanticide.

CHAPTER 5

The Right to Bear Arms

There is also an opportunity for Republicans to expand their base on the issue of the Second Amendment. According to an article in *The Guardian,* from October 30, 2020, Americans had already bought seventeen million guns so far, already setting a record for the year by September and exceeding the previous full-year record of 16.6 million in 2016. This number doesn't include the numbers for the last two months. Nor does it include people, like myself, who still haven't received their FOID card despite applying in June. What does this surge in gun buying tell you? In a year of riots, looting, burning, increasing violent crime rates, and liberal, leftist attempts to defund the police, it is screaming out one message loud and clear—government, especially in Democratic-run cities and states, either is unwilling or unable to protect its citizens. Therefore, you need to go out and get a gun to protect yourself, your family, and your businesses.

According to Statista Research in November 2020, 18 percent of Democrats personally own a gun, 31 percent of them live in a household with a gun, 29 percent of Independents personally own a gun, and 39 percent live in a household with a gun. What do these numbers tell you?

Approximately fourteen million Democrats support the Second Amendment. As the Democratic Party lurches further and further left on this issue, those voters come into play. Make no mistake about it, Democrats' ultimate goal is the repeal or total evisceration of the Second Amendment. They will start out gradually, proposing background checks, then they will seize your assault rifles, then it will be shotguns, then semiautomatic handguns, and so on and so on. Remember why the Founders included a Second Amendment in the first place. It was to prevent an absolute monarch, dictator, or government from depriving its citizens of their natural rights and liberties. That's why we fought the American Revolution.

Take a hard look at the events of 2020. Do you feel safe? Do you feel confident that the government will protect you? Even up to and throughout their National Convention, did one Democratic from Biden on down ever condemn the violence, looting, and burning? *No.* Their answer was to defund one billion dollars from the New York Police, $250,000 from the Los Angeles Police; defund the police in Seattle, Minneapolis, Portland, and countless other cities across the country. Does this make you feel safe?

The best example of what the future of the Second Amendment will be under Democrats is what happened during the riots in St. Louis, when the McCloskeys were charged by a liberal Democrat District Attorney with felonies for exercising their Second Amendment rights under the Constitution to defend themselves and their property. By the way, none of the protesters are being prosecuted.

Police across the country are being vilified. Demonizing the police is emboldening the criminals and anarchists. Most police officers are decent, good people. The few bad apples should be terminated and be put in jail when appropriate, like George Floyd's murder. They are retiring in droves, and who can blame them. Remember who it was who ran toward the Twin Towers on September 11, 2001. And just this Christmas, who ran to the RV with the bomb in it and ensured that no lives were lost in the blast? The police feel that no one appreciates them anymore. They are viewed as the bad guys instead of the ones who should be viewed that way. They are retiring in droves, and who can blame them? Does any of this make you feel safe?

Violent crime is surging in virtually every major city. Do you think this could possibly have anything to do with the lower police morale, soaring police retirements, and cutting police budgets?

Even scarier is the authoritarian, despotic control that governors and mayors have exerted over us during the COVID pandemic. I have lived on this earth in this country for nearly seventy years. I never thought that I would ever have seen anything like this in the USA. We used to be the land of the free and the home of the brave. Do you feel either free or brave? We have allowed all our freedoms to be taken away, literally overnight, without so much as a fight or even a whimper. They want us cowering in our basements. They have taken away the jobs of people deemed arbitrarily "nonessential." What gives them the right to decide who is essential? They have forced businesses to close but only businesses that they chose. They have closed our schools and our churches while leaving open liquor stores and tattoo parlors.

They have suspended the Constitution in many states, mostly blue Democratic ones. It's no wonder people are fleeing blue states, like California, New York, and Illinois, where they are being taxed and regulated to death, ordered around like children, locked down, told who they can have in their homes, and with whom they are allowed to celebrate Christmas. Make no mistake about it, this COVID exercise of raw power by Democratic governors and mayors is just a dry run for what they have planned for you in the future, especially now that Democrats are back in the White House. You've given them the key to how to control you and how to keep the masses in line. All they have to do is to scare you to death through mass hysteria. Franklin Roosevelt told us, in his first inaugural address, "You have nothing to fear but fear itself." These words were never truer than during this past year.

Why do you think that Democrats are so anxious to take your guns away? Because when they impose their radical, socialist agenda on you, you will be both incapable due to hysterical fear and unable, due to having no defenses, to do anything about it.

I implore both Democrats and Independents who still believe in the Second Amendment to watch closely which Party is protecting that right and which one is taking it away and why.

CHAPTER 6

Immigration

I previously mentioned how Joe Biden and the Democrats are planning to make fifteen million illegal immigrants into citizens so that they can vote for them. So how do the Republicans overcome this? First of all, 37 percent of Hispanics voted for Donald Trump in 2020, the highest number ever for a Republican. The Republicans must continue to advocate policies that appeal to Hispanics, such as opposition to late-term abortions, religious freedom, right to own guns, school choice in education, and jobs. They must also stress legal immigration and becoming a citizen through the normal process. One of the main reasons that so many Hispanics, especially in Florida, voted for Trump was fear of socialism. Who would know better than someone from Cuba or Venezuela, all the evils of socialism?

It is clear that the Democrats advocate open borders. They want to turn crossing the border from being a crime to a mere civil offense, and let everyone in. Who does this benefit? It benefits them—they see more future Democratic voters. It doesn't benefit Americans. We still have to pay for their education and medical care. And it takes jobs away from American workers.

What about all those immigrants who did come here legally? The ones who did it the right way and went through the long, difficult naturalization. Why should they watch people come in illegally, skip the whole process, and jump to the head do the line?

As President Trump has repeatedly said, "Without borders, you don't have a country." Which party do you want to control immigration policy? The party that wants to allow the country to be flooded with drugs, criminals, terrorists, and people to take our jobs away. Or the party that wants to keep people from illegally crossing the border, keep out drugs, criminals, and terrorists, and protect American worker's jobs.

CHAPTER 7

To My African-American Friends

A big deal was made about Donald Trump getting 12 percent of the African-American vote in 2020. While it's true that 12 percent is the most any Republican has ever received in modern political history and represented a 50 percent increase over 2016, it's still only that 12 percent, which isn't much considering that Donald Trump did more for African-Americans than any other President since Lyndon Johnson and any Republican President since Abraham Lincoln. I'm not a mathematician but that means Biden got 88 percent.

So to my Black countrymen and women, why exactly is it that you vote Democratic? What has any Democrat done to help you since Lyndon Johnson, when the Voting Rights and Civil Rights Acts of 1964 and 1965 were passed?

According to FBI statistics from 2019, the following are the US cities with most violent crimes: (1) New York, (2) Los Angeles, (3) Chicago, (4) Houston, (5) Philadelphia, (6) Memphis, (7) Detroit, (8) Dallas, (9) Phoenix, (10) Baltimore. Do you know what all those cities had in common? They were all run by Democratic mayors. And if you look at statistics for poverty rates, you will find similar results.

Just parenthetically, the only time New York City wasn't on this list was when Republican Rudy Giuliani and Republican Michael Blomberg were mayor. Forget statistics, how many of your children, spouses, mothers, fathers, grandchildren, and friends have been shot and killed since 1965? All the top urban crime cities are run by Democrats and have been so for decades. What have they done to stop crime in your neighborhoods? I'll tell you what they've done—*nothing* but give you lip service and platitudes every time right before an election comes around. I was a prosecutor for eleven years. I saw the senseless violence and blood and inhumanity and human tragedy up close. But I can never feel it like you have. Democrats have taken your votes for granted for decades and done nothing to earn or deserve them. The best example of this was when Joe Biden said, "If you have a problem figuring out whether you're for me or Trump, then you ain't Black." Those seventeen words represent the Democratic Party attitude toward Black voters for decades. Don't think about what you're doing, just vote for us like you always have. Every Black voter isn't the same, just as every white or Hispanic or Asian or Native American or any other kind of voters aren't alike. How dare they assume that you are.

I'm not telling you how to vote. This is still America for now. That's your free choice. All I'm asking you to do is to decide which Party has actually done anything for you and which hasn't. What has the man that you gave 88 percent of your votes done to help you in forty-seven years in public office? Once again—*nothing*. On the other hand, what has he done to hurt you? The answer is plenty. He opposed Clarence Thomas' going on the Supreme Court while allowing his accuser to be vilified. He joined with segregationists to block school busing, which his own Vice President pointed out during the Democratic primary debates. And by far the worst of all, he was primary force behind the passage of the 1994 Crime Bill, which resulted in the imprisonment of more African-Americans than any law in our history. With friends like this, who needs enemies.

Now, let's look at the man who 12 percent of you voted for and see why they did that and it's not because, "they ain't black." It's because he did what no Democrat had ever done for them. He, along with Senator Tim Scott, established Opportunity Zones, which encouraged investment in lower income areas. He created the Platinum Plan, which will unlock $500 million in capital into Black Communities, creating some three million jobs. He funded Historically Black Colleges for a longer period than any other president. His economy produced the lowest unemployment rate for Blacks in US history before the pandemic—5.8 percent. And here's a big one. Donald Trump got Congress to repeal the 1994 Crime Bill, which Biden got passed and never got repealed.

But to me, this is the biggest of all. What is the most important and effective way to end the cycle of poverty and violence (other than the economic opportunity which was already covered)? It's education. Again, look at the school systems in our major urban areas. Do you feel that your children are being properly educated? The answer is a resounding *no.* So why not? Because your children are stuck in underperforming schools. What's the solution? School choice. Which candidate supported school choice? It wasn't Joe Biden, who 88 percent of you voted for and who sided with the teachers' unions, who adamantly oppose school choice. It was Donald Trump who wanted you to have the right to choose what school that your children went to.

I don't know if the Republicans are smart enough to continue where Donald Trump has left off. I truly hope that they do. He has left them and you in a far better place than you were in 2016. All I'm asking is that you see what is really going on right now, determine who is acting, and not just talking. And most importantly, who is actually helping to make your lives better.

CHAPTER 8

To My Jewish Friends

I couldn't understand why Jewish voters were consistently and predominantly Democrats, so I asked several of my many Jewish friends why. The explanations seemed to center around the fact that the Jewish American experience is different from that of Israel and is based more on traditional liberalism, which they perceive to be more consistent with the Democratic Party's views. So I decided to look up the definition of liberal, and here is what I found. A liberal is someone who holds a political and social philosophy that promotes individual rights, civil liberties, democracy, and free enterprise. That pretty much squared with my personal understanding of what being a liberal is. It also encompasses the freedom to exercise your religion as you chose, which would be understandably be important to Jewish people.

You know what the problem with that is. The Democratic Party used to think that way, used to be liberal in the classic sense of the word. But sadly, that's no longer the case. Individual rights and civil liberties have given way to class distinctions, group think, conformity, and cancel culture, all of which I would think would be antithetical to Jewish beliefs.

This is not your grandfather's Democratic Party or your father's or FDR's or JFK's or even Bill Clinton's or Barack Obama's. This is a party being hijacked by radical, socialist, Marxists who don't believe in democracy, capitalism, individual rights, freedom of speech, or religion. Socialism and Marxism are secular. They don't contemplate religion having a place in their society. That can't be what Jewish people want.

Also this new radical Democratic Party has shown that what they really want is more government control over everything. They've demonstrated what the future holds by how they've handled the pandemic. They will lock you down while they violate their own rules. Look what they did to churches in general and the Jews in New York in particular. Is this liberalism? Or totalitarianism?

Finally, let's talk taxes. Joe Biden and the Democrats have made no secret about what they will do to the wealthy—tax you to death. Take your money and give free handouts and things to groups just to buy their votes, calling it "redistribution of wealth." It's your wealth they're planning on redistributing that you worked so hard to get. And what about estate taxes? After Donald Trump made it easier for you and everyone else to pass on their wealth to their kids and grandkids, what do you think Biden and the Democrats are going to do when they get power? They are going to reinstate huge estate taxes on you.

According to a PEW Research Center Survey, ending in June 2020, 71 percent of American Jews are Democrats, while only 26 percent lean Republican. I would ask those 71 percent if the party they support is still the liberal party it used to be.

Although you might not totally support the Conversative Likud party Israel, you can't deny that Donald Trump was a far better friend to Israel than Obama/Biden were. Trump recognized Jerusalem as Israel's capital, which American presidents have been promising to do for decades but never had the guts to. He moved the US embassy to Jerusalem and recognized Israel's right to the Golan Heights. More importantly, he redefined the dynamic in the Middle East and brokered peace deals between Israel and four Arab countries—Bahrain, Morocco, United Arab Emirates, and Sudan.

And don't forget the anti-Semitic rhetoric being spewed by Democrats Ilhan Omar and Rashid Talib and then being condoned by Nancy Pelosi, allowing anti-Semite Linda Sarsour to speak at the Democratic National Convention; backing anti-Semitic groups such as Antifa and BLM.

What awaits you under four years of Joe Biden is more of the same anti-Semitic rhetoric and anti-Israel policies.

CHAPTER 9

The Media

The media is a primary force behind the impending death of the Republican Party.

When the Founders put freedom of the press in the First Amendment, they did so for a reason. They recognized the role that a free and independent press should play in protecting democracy. The press is supposed to question, probe, investigate, challenge ideas, inform but do so independently. It is the "independent" part that seems to have been lost somewhere along the way.

Remember when the press led the way in the fight against fascism and totalitarianism during WWII, when it exposed the senselessness of the Vietnam War, when Woodward and Bernstein exposed Watergate; when Walter Cronkite "the most trusted man in America" told us every weeknight, "And that's the way it is." How about Edward R. Murrow, Huntley and Brinkley, Frank Reynolds, Harry Reasoner, and Hugh Downs. Can you see any one those respected Titans of the industry saying and doing the things that the current lightweights on CNN, CNBC, ABC, CBS, NBC, N.Y. Times, and Washington Post are spewing out?

This all started slowly, back during the Ronald Reagan years, when the press attacked him as senile and too conservative. He fended it off with humor and laughed it off. But that was just the start. The eight years under George W. Bush were rock bottom, I thought at the time. Boy, was I wrong. Bush just took it and didn't fight back. Then, there were the attacks on John McCain in 2008 and Mitt Romney in 2012, again taken without resistance. Do you notice a pattern here as to which is the only Party being attacked by the "independent" press?

Then came the eight-year love fest with Obama/Biden, who apparently did nothing worth attacking. All this set up the main course—the all-out war on Donald Trump. Never in the history of the country or politics or the press has there been such a purposeful, concentrated, biased attack against one politician. This was a headline on January 20, 2017, the very day that Donald Trump was sworn in:

"The Campaign to impeach President Trump has begun."

Think about that for a second. On the day that Donald Trump took office, one of the supposedly most prestigious newspapers in the country is advocating impeaching a US President before he has even performed one official act as president. Does that sound independent and unbiased to you? And things just went downhill from there. Every day since that day, the sole purpose of the news and print media, social media, The Democratic Party, the deep state, RINO Republicans, and the swamp in DC was to remove Donald Trump from Office by any means necessary. And I mean precisely that—by any means.

What caused this irrational hatred of one man? Donald Trump was an outsider. He wasn't "one of them." He was like a giant alligator thrashing around in the swamp, disrupting the natural order of things. He couldn't be controlled. No one knew what he would do next. This wasn't supposed to happen. This couldn't be allowed to stand. Hillary was supposed to win so that all their misdeeds would be covered up—their spying on Trump's campaign and presidency, the fake Steel dossier, and the Trump colluded with Russia hoax. The Democrats and their enablers in the media never accepted the results of the 2016 election, never regarded Donald Trump as a legitimate president, and blamed and looked down on the "smelly Walmart shoppers" who voted for Trump.

Every day, each soldier in the media army woke up with one thought—How can we make Donald Trump look bad today? How soon can we figure out some way to get rid of him? What grounds can we come up with to impeach him on? Unfortunately, Donald Trump's tweets often gave them free ammunition. But when there was nothing else to use against him, no problem, they just made stuff up or used leaked "anonymous sources."

When their savior Robert Muller didn't come up with the goods to impeach Trump on the Russia collusion hoax, the media and Democrats really started to panic. They were running out of time. So they next turned a perfectly legitimate phone call to the President of Ukraine into an illegitimate impeachment. Once again, the media was right there leading the way, pushing another hoax. What was most frustrating and revealing was that the media had help on this one from the deep state and the swamp. The FBI had possession of Hunter Biden's laptop in late 2019. President Trump was impeached on December 18, 2019. Do you know what that means? Hunter Biden's laptop provided all the justification and evidence that was needed to justify any and all requests to investigate the Bidens. The FBI sat on and withheld evidence that would have justified all of Donald Trump's actions. They sat by silently and allowed an invalid impeachment to proceed, knowing that there were perfectly legitimate reasons for both Ukraine and our Department of Justice to investigate Hunter Biden. Funny how there were no leaks about this, despite anonymous leaks coming out on every single thing that hurt Donald Trump for four years.

In 1942, then Vice President Henry A. Wallace compared fascism to an "infectious disease" and warned against the "deliberate, systematic poisoning of public channels of information." He must have been a fortune-teller and predictor of the future. Wallace's worst fears have been realized. That is exactly what the mainstream press has become—a deliberate and systematic poisoner of all information that the public receives. They really are "fake news," as Donald Trump calls them. All of them—The Washington Post, The N.Y. Times, CNN, CNBC, ABC, CBS, NBC have become arms of the Democratic Party. They slant the news to fit the Democratic agenda, or they simply ignore everything negative about Democrats.

Negative press coverage of Donald Trump rose from 91 percent to 95 percent according to a study released on August 17, 2020, by the Media Research Center. This is unheard of and confirms the media's clear bias in favor of Democrats. In a Gallup poll released on August 4, 2020, nearly 54 percent of Americans believe that reporters are "misrepresenting the facts" and 28 percent believe that reporters are "making facts up entirely."

The mainstream media is just state-run propaganda TV for the Democratic Party. It is just like Iran's Islamic Republic of Iran Broadcasting (IRIB), North Korea's Central Television (KCTV), the Russia Television and Radio Broadcasting Network, or China Central Television (CCTV).

The question is what can be done about it? Who can and will hold the media accountable? The answer is you. Hit them where it hurts. Cancel your subscription to the Washington Post and N.Y. Times. Stop watching CNN, CNBC, and the national broadcasts of ABC, NBC, and CBS. Get your news from the local TV stations, which aren't as biased. Tell them that you're not coming back until they start acting like an independent press and treat both Parties the same. Otherwise, we'll be just be a one-party system with Democratic state-run TV.

CHAPTER 10

Big Tech and Section 230

Although the Big Tech giants of Facebook, Twitter, Google, and YouTube are technically part of the larger media, their actions are so egregious that they deserve their own chapter. Big Tech is part of the state-run Democratic propaganda machine to be sure. Their blatant censorship is far more prevalent and sinister than that of the mainstream press.

Just to give some perspective, in the 2020 election, 95 percent of people working in Big Tech contributed to Democrats, which goes a long way in explaining their actions.

Let's have a history lesson. Facebook was formed in 2004, Google in 1998, YouTube in 2006, and Twitter in 2006. When they were just nascent, struggling companies, they needed help getting off the ground. So who came to their rescue? Congress, of course, in the form of Section 230 of the Communication Decency Act of 1996. Section 230 says that online platforms are not legally responsible for what users post. The so-called "Good Samaritan" provision, Section 230 prevents them from being sued by users if they "act in good faith to restrict access to or availability of material that the provider or user considers to be obscene, lewd, lascivious, lewd, filthy, excessively violent, harassing, or otherwise objectionable, whether or not such material is constitutionally protected." So here's the problem. Tech companies are no longer merely platforms, like telephone companies are, where users can say what they please without being censored. No one interrupts your phone calls to stop you from saying anything that you want. That is a platform. Tech companies like Twitter, Facebook, YouTube, and Google are no longer merely platforms. They selectively choose who to suspend or ban. That is performing the function of an editor or publisher. They should no longer be afforded the protections of Section 230.

Big Tech routinely censors free speech but almost exclusively in one direction—against Conservatives. Twitter and Facebook are by far the greatest transgressors.

The most glaring example was how they handled the Hunter Biden's laptop issue. When news broke in the *Washington Post* in mid-October, 2020 about Hunter's email and laptop, what happened and what didn't happen? What didn't happen at first was any mention of it in the fake news media at all, as they faithfully performed their role as arm of the Democratic Party and protector of Joe Biden. When they did mention it, they called it "Russian disinformation," another lie perpetrated by the media, as if somehow emails taken directly from Hunter Biden's own laptop had anything to do with Russia. So what did Big Tech do? Twitter's Jack Dorsey and Facebook's Marc Zuckerberg immediately banned any mention by anybody of the *Post* article. The *Post* is the nation's fifth largest newspaper, and their article was banned from Twitter and Facebook. Just think about that. What unrestrained power! Whatever happened to freedom of speech and the press? They seem to only apply when they help Democrats.

Unfortunately, it didn't stop there. When former Biden associate, Tony Bobulinski, came out with his public statement on October 22, 2020, accompanied by emails, phone calls, and documents as corroboration, he was likewise ignored by the fake news media and banned from Twitter. As Bobulinski himself said, "The deep state is trying to silence me." And the sad thing is that it worked. In post-election polls, estimates ranging from 33–45 percent of Biden voters never heard anything about Hunter Biden's laptop or emails before the election. The media and Big Tech did their jobs well. In several polls conducted post-election, upwards of 3 percent of Biden voters in the swing states said that, if they had known about Hunter Biden's laptop and emails, they would either have voted for Trump or not voted at all. That fact alone would have directly impacted the election.

CHAPTER 11

Global Warming/Climate Change

You may be wondering why I've included a chapter on global warming and climate change. Well, there's a method to my madness. All you hear from Democrats and their experts is that global warming is an "existential threat." An existential threat is defined as an event that could cause human extinction or is a threat to our very existence. That sounds pretty serious, doesn't it? Pretty scary stuff! And that's exactly the point. It's purposely designed to scare the hell out of you. I'm not here to tell you to listen to me or experts on either side of this issue. I'm asking you to investigate and decide for yourself. You should realize by now that you can't just listen to the press or so-called experts or politicians like AOC or Bernie Sanders or an eighteen-year-old from Sweden. Do your own research as I did. This is what I found.

You can accept it or not as you choose. Global warming and climate change have been happening throughout geologic time. There have been periods of extreme hot and extreme cold. This just didn't start after the Industrial Revolution. The fact is that there have been thirty-four separate periods of glacial melting throughout history. The simple truth is that we cannot determinatively control climate change or global warming, even if we reduced carbon emissions to zero. And we don't want to totally reduce carbon emissions to zero because plants and trees need it to survive. The fact is that in 2019, carbon emissions in the US declined nearly 3 percent and since 2000, the US has had the largest decline in carbon emissions relating to energy use of any other country. We aren't the problem, China is.

That brings to the Paris Climate Accord, which President Trump rightly withdrew from. First of all, it's totally voluntary, there's no enforcement mechanism. Second, we were committing the most money to it, as always. Third, we have been doing just great reducing our carbon emissions since we left it. Finally, China doesn't have to reach peak carbon emission until 2030. It's just symbolic and a costly one at that. There's absolutely no reason to totally eliminate fossil fuels (coal, oil, and natural gas). As we've proven over the past four years, we keep them and still reduce carbon as long we develop cleaner coal, use fracking to produce natural gas which is cleaner, and increase nuclear power.

Our economy is too dependent on fossil fuels to eliminate them altogether. It would devastate the economies of many states. We had been energy independent for the first time in decades under Donald Trump. Do we really want to change that? We can do both—keep using fossil fuels cleanly as possible and supplement them with solar, wind, electric vehicles, and geothermal. So what's behind the Democrats' big push for the Green New Deal, banning fracking, and elimination of all fossil fuels? My advice is to follow the money. It always provides the answer. When an expert tells you that global warming demands elimination of all fossil fuels, look into his background. For whom does he work? Who is supplying his grants? Check what companies are making donations to the politicians that are most strongly backing it. See what companies will gain the most by passage of the Green New Deal.

By the way, have you ever actually read the entire Green New Deal? It's pretty revealing. It's nothing more than a total expansion of the role of the federal government, a complete takeover of our lives by government—

telling us what vehicles to drive, what kind of houses to live in, what food to eat, what transportation we can take, whether we can own cows. It leads to socialism and totalitarianism, where we the masses are all sheep being told how to live. Not to mention the $93 trillion cost. No need to question them—they'll give you everything for free. Just trust them. The problem is nothing is for free—somebody has to pay. And it will be you!

The COVID lockdowns were just a dry run for the next "existential crisis global warming." They have the blueprint in place now, at least in Democratic blue states. Scare everyone to death, have the media work everyone into a frenzy. Then, the sheep will be so afraid, they will accept everything that they're told. They give up all their freedoms, their jobs, their businesses, their families, their friends, their holidays, their sports, their gyms, and their freedom of speech and religion. The global warming lockdowns and restrictions are next. All I'm asking is to don't believe anyone, me included, without questioning or investigating. Just go out and decide for yourself.

CHAPTER 12

Conservative Core Values and the Trump Coalition

To have any chance to survive, the Republican Party must get back to core conservative values. They were laid out by Ronald Reagan and expanded by Donald Trump—smaller role for federal government, free enterprise, lower taxes, trickle-down economy, strong military, less government spending, fewer regulations, strong border and immigration policy, 2nd Amendment right to bear arms, and right to life (especially late-term). Donald Trump added America First, better trade deals, taking on China, and patriotism. Partly due to the pandemic, Republicans were forced to get away from reduced spending and reduced role of government. Republicans need to hold to their core values and draw a clear contrast with the Democrats.

Trump transformed the Republican Party into a populist, working-class, rural party. In 2020, he captured 57 percent of the white vote, 32 percent of the Hispanic vote, and 12 percent of the Black vote. The question is can anyone else besides Donald Trump hold this coalition together? Trump's supporters are fiercely loyal to him. When have you ever seen followers at a presidential rally chant, "We love you" to a candidate? Donald Trump was a generational figure, a political outsider, who gave a voice to so many who had felt ignored for so long.

I felt that it was highly questionable that anyone could recapture the feelings that Trump's supporters had for him even before the events of the first week of January 2021. That was the week that the undoing of the Trump legacy and the Elephant. First, Trump's magic couldn't save either of the Georgia Senate seats. Second, the assault on the Capitol hurt the very cause that brought all those protesters there in the first place. No one will remember or care about anything besides the images of the "insurrection."

All this will make it even more difficult for even Donald Trump and certainly anyone else, to keep that fragile coalition from evaporating.

CHAPTER 13

Hypocrisy, Double Standards, and a Two-Tier Justice System

To say that Democrats and the fake news media are hypocrites with double standards is the understatement of the century.

Let's start out by going back to the election of 2016. After openly crying on TV when Donald Trump won the election in 2016, the fake news began their four-year refusal to accept the results of the election. They claimed Donald Trump was an illegitimate president right then and never stopped saying it. In the 19 minutes after Donald Trump was sworn in on January 20, 2017, the *Washington Post* ran a headline saying that "The impeachment of Donald Trump has begun." The Democrats and their pals in the media tried to remove him with a series of "trumped-up conspiracies" from Russian collusion to Ukraine to Stormy Daniels.

Hillary Clinton never acknowledged she lost. Neither did Stacey Abrams in Georgia. But that was perfectly okay. Why? Because they were Democrats. However, when Donald Trump and Republicans dare to do the very same thing in 2020, they are evil and committing sedition. There are legitimate concerns about the integrity of the 2020 election and anyone, Democrat or Republican, who tells you otherwise is lying to you. There were hundreds of affidavits filed by whistleblowers in all the six major contested swing states, but for some reason, no one wanted to listen to them.

Do you remember how differently the Democrats and their lackeys in the media reacted when a supposed whistleblower leaked Donald Trump's phone call to the president of Ukraine? They praised the courage of whistleblowers and proclaimed that they should all be believed. What was the difference? Well, one was accusing a Republican and therefore should be believed, and the other hundreds were accusing Democrats and therefore are liars and should be dismissed and ignored. There are also legitimate legal and constitutional issues in several states, which will be discussed in further detail in Chapter 14.

Remember what Hillary Clinton's advice to Joe Biden was before the election of 2020? "Don't concede under any circumstances. Fight to the end." Which is exactly what Biden would have done had the outcome been reversed. He had his team of hundreds of lawyers all ready to go. That was exactly what Al Gore did in 2020, taking his case to the US Supreme Court twice before finally losing. Gore had the full support of the Democrats and media back then.

Does anyone remember Nancy Pelosi's tweet in early 2017? "Our election was hijacked. There is no question. Congress has a duty to #Protect Our Democracy & Follow the Facts." Did anyone have a problem with that one? Of course not. What's the difference now when Donald Trump contests the election? There is no difference except for the double standard. Now, when Trump does it, it suddenly becomes sedition.

Want more examples of hypocrisy and double standards? Let's go back to 1998, when the Republicans impeached Bill Clinton. What did the Democrats say back then? Senator Leahy said, "Partisan impeachment drives are doomed to fail." Senator Ed Markey (D-Mass) said that Congress was at the "threshold of overturning the people's choice for president." Senator Chuck Schumer (D-NY) said that the GOP-led Senate could turn the trial into a nationally televised meeting of the mock trial club. They then turned around in 2019 and did exactly what they were complaining about in 1998.

Now to even more heights of Democratic hypocrisy. Democrats have accused Republican Congressman or Senators who voiced objections to the Electoral College vote as being seditious and encouraging violence. This is preposterous. First of all, they have a First Amendment right of freedom speech. But more importantly, they were doing exactly what Democrats did in the 2000 election, the 2004 election, and the 2016 election. In early January 2005, Senator Barbara Boxer (D-Ohio), along with Rep. Stephanie Tubbs (D-Ohio), objected to Bush's 2004 electoral votes in Ohio. Back then, Nancy Pelosi praised her challenge, saying, "Today, we are witnessing Democracy in action. This isn't as some of our Republican colleagues have referred to it, sadly, as frivolous. This debate is fundamental to our democracy."

Why isn't what Senators Hawley and Cruz and over 100 Republican members objecting in 2020 similarly fundamental to our democracy? I'll tell you why. Because Democrats are hypocritical with double standards. Let's take a look at the 2016 election. On January 6, 2017, seven House Democrats tried or object to electors from multiple states: Jim McGovern (D-Mass.) objected to Alabama's votes. Jamie Raskin (D-Md.) objected to Florida's votes.

Pramila Jayapal (D-Wash) objected to Georgia's votes. Sheila Jackson (D-Tx) objected to votes from South Carolina and Wisconsin. Barbara Lee (D-Cal) objected to Michigan's votes. Paul Grijalva (D-Ariz.) objected to Arizona's votes and Maxine Waters (D-Cal.) objected too. In the 2000 election, several Democratic members of the House likewise objected to the electors in Florida.

Apparently, what's good for the Democratic goose isn't good for the Republican gander. The other point is that have you heard anything about the Democratic prior objections from the fake news?

Now, let's talk about the two-tiered justice system that Kamala Harris claims exists in America. Kamala is right about there being a two-tiered justice system. However, it's not based on race. It's based on party affiliation. If you're a Democrat, you get off. Take Hilary Clinton. The Democratic FBI cleared her of any wrongdoing in her email scandal, before talking to her or any witnesses. Then, those same FBI agents used the fake Steele Hillary Clinton/DNC bought dossier to get FISA warrants to spy on Donald Trump and his campaign. It gets better. Inspector General Michael Horowitz recommended criminal referrals for James Comey for leaking and Andrew McCabe for lying four times.

Were any charges filed against either one? Of course not. The deep state and the swamp protect each other. Let's look at what happened to Trump Republicans. George Papadopoulos, a low-level advisor to Trump's 2016 campaign, spent twelve days in jail for making allegedly false statements to the FBI, whom he claims (and the newly-released evidence supports) entrapped him. Roger Stone, long-time Trump ally, charged with lying to Congress and other crimes, has his house raided in the middle of the night by dozens of armed FBI agents and somehow, CNN shows up. And then there's General Michael Flynn, Trump's National Security Adviser. He was charged with perjury, even though Comey and Peter Strzok's own FBI agents said he didn't lie, just so that they could try to get to Donald Trump.

If Democrats didn't have double standards, they wouldn't have any standards at all.

CHAPTER 14

It's All Up to You, Joe

It's all up to Joe now—*no,* not that Joe in the White House. The other Joe—Joe Manchin Democratic Senator from West Virginia. Now that the Democrats have control of the Senate due to the Republicans losing both runoffs in Georgia, it would appear that the table is set for Chuck Schumer's, "First, we take Georgia, then we change America" slogan to come true. Here are some of the proposed changes: packing the Supreme Court with judicial activists, adding DC and Puerto Rico as states to give Democrats four more Senators, open borders, defunding the police, the Green New Deal, Medicare for all, just to name a few. There's nothing to stop them now except for Joe Manchin.

Joe has publicly stated twice firmly that he would not vote to end the filibuster, which would open up Pandora's box for Democrats. Manchin feels that the filibuster is what makes the Senate different from the House, and he's right. The filibuster forces compromise, instead of one-party excesses and domination. Joe is a moderate by Democratic standards. He insists that he is still a "proud Democrat." The question that I have for Joe is this, "How can you be proud to be in the same party as AOC, Rashid Talib, Ilan Omar, Maxine Waters, Eric Swalwell, Jerry Nadler, Adam Schiff, Nancy Pelosi, Chuck Schumer, Elizabeth Warren, Bernie Sanders, and now the Socialists, Warnock and Ossoff, just to name a few?"

Manchin will come under tremendous attack by all these and more if he sticks to his guns. The reality is that many of Joe Manchin's views are more in line with Republicans than Democrats. Given the ostracizing that he is in for by his intolerant fellow Democrats, maybe Joe should follow the lead of now Republicans Jeff Van Drew and Vernon Jones among others and switch parties. Whether he does or not, Manchin's vote is critical to stemming the power grab by the Democrats and their attempt to eliminate the Republican Party altogether and implement their radical, socialist agenda.

The other factor at play here is that West Virginia has become of the reddest states in the country and is coal country. The Democrats are hell-bent on eliminating fossil fuels especially coal. This would cripple West Virginia's economy and send it back to the Dark Ages. So Joe, for the sake of the country and your precious West Virginia, hold the line!

CHAPTER 15

The Final Nail in the Coffin

The final nail in the elephant's coffin is mail-in balloting. Unless this is fixed, there will never be another Republican elected president. After the election of 2020, Democrats have the blueprint for all future elections. The simple truth is that mail-in ballots are fraught with security issues and potential for fraud. Don't take my word for it.

Let's start with an article in *The N.Y. Times* from October 6, 2012, titled "Error and Fraud at Issue as Absentee Voting Rises." The article states,

> Absentee ballots have been rejected in Minnesota and elsewhere for count-less reasons. Signatures for older people, sloppy writers or stroke victims may not

match those on file. The envelope and forms may not been configured in the right sequence. People may have moved and addresses may not match. Witnesses may not be registered to vote. The mail may be late.

Heather Gerken, a law professor at Yale, stated in that same article,

> You could steal some absentee ballots or stuff a ballot box or bribe, an election administrator, or fiddle with an electronic voting machine. That explains why all the evidence of stolen elections involves absentee ballots and the like.

Even more significantly, Former President Jimmy Carter and James Baker cochaired a Commission on Election Integrity in 2005. Despite Carter's present attempts to discredit his own report to support the Democratic Party line in 2020, this is what his report said in 2005 about mail-in ballots in Section 4.2 titled, "Vote by Mail."

Vote by mail raises concerns about privacy, as citizens voting at home may come under pressure to vote for certain candidates, and it increase the risk of fraud. Vote by mail is, however, likely to increase the risks of fraud and of contested elections in other states (besides Oregon), where the population is mobile, where there is a history of turbulent elections, or where the safeguards for ballot integrity are weaker.

These statements from Carter's 2005 report were still valid in the 2020 election and going forward, especially given the sheer volume of mail-in ballots in 2020, and the number of states doing it for the very first time. Compounding this was the fact that five states, like Nevada, just sent out two million mail-in ballots to everyone without purging their voter records. Anyone being objective can see the potential for fraud here. Voters may have moved, they may be dead, or the ballots may be stolen. Why take that chance?

In person voting is the safest way to decrease fraud. The voter comes in, shows his or her ID, the poll watcher can see it's really them, they sign in front of them, and the signatures are compared. There's no safer way. People do occasionally need absentee ballots. Just to be clear, there is a difference between absentee ballots and mail-in ballots. All states have procedures for people who know ahead of time that they can't vote on election day. Procedural safeguards are set up. The voter must request a ballot. The number is relatively small compared to mail-in ballots. There is no mass influx of ballots. I understand that in 2020,COVID-19 safety concerns necessitated a change for that election only. There is no reason to keep doing it on that scale any further. You have ballot harvesting concerns, where one person collects the ballots for hundreds of voters and then drops them in drop boxes or in the mail. Who knows what these individuals are actually doing with all those ballots.

That then brings up the issue of drop boxes, another area of potential fraud if not done correctly. Such drop boxes must have 24 hour cameras, and be placed only in secure locations, such as early-voting polling places or police stations or near government buildings. Ironically, Illinois, which gets nothing else right, got mail-in voting right. In Illinois, they first sent out ballot applications to voters, not the ballots themselves. Voters then had to send back the signed application with both proof of residency and a photo ID from that address. This process at least allows verification that the person actually lives there, is who he or she says they are, and allows signature verification with the one on file. Unfortunately, that's not what happened in most states.

For example, in Georgia, photo IDs were required for in-person voters but not for mail-in ones. Why not? In Wisconsin, three members of the Wisconsin State Supreme Court found that Wisconsin had violated its own election laws relating to mail-in ballots and couldn't understand how the other four justices allowed this to stand and didn't strike the votes. In Pennsylvania, there was inconsistent application of the "curing" policies for defective mail-in ballots for Democrats and Republicans. State election officials changed the policies and allowed voters to be notified and correct errors in the mail-in ballots prior to election.

The problem is, this policy was not applied consistently or equally. Democrats notified their voters to cure their defective mail-in ballots while many Republican counties didn't because they felt that the curing policy was unconstitutional, which it may very well have been especially if applied unequally. Pennsylvania Democratic state election officials and their Democratic State Supreme Court further violated the US Constitution by extending the date to accept mail-in ballots after November 3, in contradiction to the Pennsylvania State Legislature which has the sole power to do so.

No fair person can conclude that there weren't issues with relying so heavily on mail-in ballots for the first time in many states, in a high turnout presidential election. It took Washington and Oregon several election cycles to get all the kinks out. If the Republican state legislatures, whose duty it is under the US Constitution, don't fix the process for mail-in ballots before 2022 and 2024, there will never be another Republican elected president. I didn't mention Democratic state legislatures because they will never change a system that worked for them, tainted or not. Photo IDs must be required for both in-person and mail-in ballots. Signature comparison with the signature on file must be mandated. All ballots must be received by election day to be counted. Only state legislatures, not election or state officials even governors or judges, should regulate how elections are held.

Finally, there needs to be an Independent Election Commission appointed to investigate the 2020 election and propose changes to ensure election integrity. Everyone should want and support this unless they have something to hide.

CHAPTER 16

In God We Trust

The Pledge of Allegiance was written in 1892. It was adopted in 1942, and actually named "The Pledge of Allegiance" in 1945. The words "under God" were put in in 1954. "In God We Trust" was put on our coins in 1938 and added to all currency in 1956. It became our national motto in 1957. Our precious rights of life, liberty, and the pursuit of happiness have always been regarded as God-given natural rights. As I look around the county and the world, I see a very disturbing trend—attacks on religion are on the rise everywhere. Christians are being persecuted in Africa and Asia. Muslims are being interned in camps in China. Anti-Semitic attacks occur frequently in the US, as do anti-Semitic comments by Democratic politicians in the House.

During Amy Coney Barret's confirmation to the US Court of Appeals, she was brutally and verbally attacked for being a devout Catholic. Two separate caucuses during the 2020 Democratic Convention read the Pledge of Allegiance without saying words "under God." At the 111th Golf US Open, NBC had school children recite the Pledge of Allegiance twice without saying "under God." So did a teacher in California. These are just snippets of what's happening all over the country. A silent, under-the-radar attack on God and religion by Democrats, liberals, socialists, and their media partners.

I was raised a Catholic. I went to Catholic grammar school and high school. I then strayed from organized religion. I am now realizing that's exactly what the country is doing. Why this conscious push toward secularism and away from religion? Why are churches deemed non-essential and closed during the pandemic and liquor stores allowed to stay open? Why does Nancy Pelosi use her Catholic religion as a shield when it suits her political purposes and then advocate killing babies up to the moment of birth? What ever happened to family values? I'll tell you precisely why this is all happening.

The Democratic Party has moved so far to the left, that is now indistinguishable from socialism and is steaming headlong toward outright Marxism and totalitarianism.

And do you know what there is no room for in Marxism? God and religion. Marxism and totalitarianism are secular societies and forms of government. The State is their religion. You give homage to the State, not God. The State provides for all your needs and controls all aspects of your life. This is why the left-wing socialist Democrats need to eliminate religion and God as a first step toward their ultimate goal. All I'm asking is for you to be aware of what's happening and to look for the little signs, the snippets that might not seem much on their own, by taken together. Get back to traditional family values, to religion, and God, by whatever name you call him. It's the only answer.

CHAPTER 17

The Donkey

Lest Democrats feel slighted, I'll now turn my attention to them. This is not the Democratic Party we are all used to. It has now moved so far left that Bill Clinton and Barack Obama have been "left" behind. Democrats are the party of the Green New Deal, Medicare for all, open borders, abolish ICE, sanctuary cites, defund the police, identity politics, reduced military spending, eliminating fossil fuels, America last, losing jobs overseas, kowtowing to China, and bad trade deals. More importantly, they are the party of groupthink, censorship, and cancel culture. They no longer believe in free market capitalism or freedom of speech. As such, they should properly abandon the name Democratic because "democratic" they aren't. They should rename themselves the Socialist or Progressive Party. As far as their symbol of the donkey, in many ways that still fits. Donkeys are stubborn and stupid, just like the Democratic Party leadership. But I have another suggestion for their symbol—the Pig.

"The left wing of the party wants to defund the police," before "so what could be more fitting" so what could be more fitting. There's another, even better, reason why the pig is the answer. George Orwell's novel, *Animal Farm,* is widely recognized as a parody of the Russian Revolution. Since the Democrats are turning our country into the USSR, what could be more appropriate? At the end of Animal Farm, Napoleon the Pig became the dictator of the Farm. So I vote for the pig as the Democratic Party's new symbol.

This is now meant for the Democratic voters, not the left-wing socialists, because you are too far gone to be reasoned with. This is for the moderate Democrats and even Independents. I know that you hated Donald Trump and wanted him out. There was a lot to dislike about him I admit. His tweets, his tone, his brashness, his harsh language, his personality, and his demeanor. Having a president who is likeable and kind is important because words do matter. But consider this. What's more important, words or actions? Tone or results? Jimmy Carter was one of the kindest, most mild-mannered presidents ever, not a mean bone in his body. What were his results? He was one of the worst presidents we ever had, both domestically and internationally.

You've voted out the evil one responsible for everything bad in the country because of his words and behavior. But what about his actions, his results? He gave us the greatest economy we've ever had, the lowest unemployment rate in sixty years, the lowest unemployment rate for Blacks, Hispanics, Asians, youth, and women ever; rising wages, lower poverty rate, energy independence for the first time in sixty years, strong borders, law and order, a strong military, lower taxes, reduced regulations that were strangling businesses, better trade deals, confronted China, forced NATO countries to start paying their fair share, destroyed the ISIS caliphate, appointed judge who will interpret the law, not make it; brought jobs back to America from overseas, revived manufacturing, and revived the steel and coal industries, all while lowering carbon levels.

But you may not realize it now, but what you'll miss most about Donald Trump is his unabashed patriotism, his love of the country, his putting America first, instead of last; his belief that America, although flawed, is still the greatest country that God ever put on this earth and not some evil, systemically racist country that Democrats would have you believe. Be careful what you wish for because you just don't know what you're going to get. Although in this situation, as I look into my crystal ball, I can pretty much tell you exactly what you're going to get.

You're in store for more government control over your life; runaway government spending; higher taxes; open borders with drugs, criminals, and terrorists pouring in and illegals taking your jobs; liberal, activist judges; your guns being taken away; no more energy independence; elimination of coal, oil, and natural gas; loss of manufacturing jobs to overseas; complete submission to Chinese takeover; lockdowns as a first option, America last; a weaker military; defunding the police and no-bail laws causing higher crime; killing babies up to the moment of birth; no school choice; and worst of all, censorship and cancel culture running wild.

Yes, be careful what you wish for. All I'm asking you to do is to sit back and watch what happens and see if I'm right. We'll talk in 2024. At that point, ask yourselves, "Am I better off than I was on January 1, 2020, before COVID hit?"

CHAPTER 18

Killing the Elephant

For most of this book, I have been discussing the slow, inevitable death of the Republican Party. As I was finishing the book, something critical happened—January 6, 2021— the storming of the Capitol. That changed everything. The short-sighted anarchists and criminals who did that severely hurt the cause of both the hundreds of thousands who had come to peacefully protest the election that day, and the 74 million people who had voted for Donald Trump. They also prevented the Congressmen and Senators from making their objections to the electors in the Capitol that day. This was a dreadful day for the country, and an even worse one for the Republican Party.

But the Democrats are never ones to let a crisis go to waste. They created another impeachment hoax, this one in record speed. The purpose of impeachment is to remove the president from office. Donald Trump is no longer in office after January 20, 2021. So how can you remove someone from office who is no longer in office anymore?

Setting that aside for a moment, the single article of impeachment states that Trump incited violence in his speech on January 6, 2021. There are two problems with this. First, Trump never incited anything during in his speech. What he said was that he knew that they were going to march to the Capitol and peacefully and patriotically protest. Even more importantly is that more information has come out since the House hastily impeached the President. The FBI has revealed that it had obtained information from social media and other law enforcement agencies that an attack on the Capitol was being planned days before January 6, 2021. The anarchists apparently had planted items for the attack around the city and retrieved them when needed.

So one might wonder how President Trump could incite an insurrection in a speech that was made after the attack was already planned out. The simple truth is that this impeachment, just like the first one, was nothing more than a political ploy to further discredit Donald Trump. This one is clearly an attempt to prevent him from running again in 2024. All ten Republican House members who voted to impeach the

President should be primaried in 2022 and defeated. They have defied the wishes of Republicans in their districts and states and divided the Republican Party. The same goes for any Senator who voted to convict. If this impeachment hoax had been the only thing that Democrat and their allies in the media had pulled after the January 6 attacks (which should be condemned by everyone) that would have been bad enough. But they were just getting started.

I have never been more afraid for the country as I am now. Never in our history has there been such a consolidation of powerful forces arrayed against an individual or a political party as there are today. Not only do the Democrats control the Executive and both houses of the Legislative Branch, but they are plotting to expand the Supreme Court with judicial activists, so they can control Third Branch, the Judiciary. They have 99 percent of the media as basically an arm of the Democratic Party—their own state-run media. Big Tech social media are their allies as well. Throw in Wall Street, Globalist corporations, the swamp, the deep state, RINO Republicans, the entertainment industry, sports, and what's left?

All these forces are now using the Capitol attacks to set their sights on killing the Elephant, destroying not just Donald Trump but his Populist coalition, the entire Republican Party, the conservatives, and all 74 million

Trump supporters. If you think that I'm exaggerating, then you're not paying attention to what's happening in the country.

First, both Twitter and Facebook banned President Trump. Twitter also banned 80,000 conservative Trump supporters. Twitter, Facebook, Amazon, Google, Apple, and others effectively knocked the libertarian, conservative social network service and app Parler off-line. Several large companies, have suspended donations to all Republicans who objected to the 2020 Electoral vote. So much for free speech. Incidentally, no such action was taken against any Democrats who similarly objected to the Electoral College vote in 2000, 2004, and 2016. It goes on. Numerous fake news commentators on places such CNN and other all across the media are calling all Trump supporters racists and Nazis. They are calling for Trump supporters to be "reprogrammed."

They are engaging in censorship and trying to cancel any opinion that disagrees with them. Is this the America that you want to live in? Be careful, they will be coming for you next. Once the Democrats have killed the Elephant, where does their yellow brick road take us? Not to the Emerald City or a city on a hill. It takes us to totalitarianism, to socialism, and to Marxism, where there is only one party. It takes us to Iran, to North Korea, to the USSR, or to China.

It takes us to Oceania, from George Orwell's *1984,* a totalitarian state where Big Brother is always watching you, and the Thought Police come after anyone who has independent thoughts. Starting to sound familiar? What was once thought to be science fiction is now starting to turn into reality. Winston Smith, Orwell's protagonist, is taken to Rm 10, where he is "reeducated" into the party line. Then, there's the Ministry of Truth, where all photographs and records of people who have been erased from history are destroyed. Doesn't this sound all too similar to Twitter and Facebook permanently banning conservatives and the fake news all calling for Trump supporters to be "re-programmed?" Go read or reread *1984* before it's too late because that's where those now in power are taking us.

There is a ray of hope. It's in Chapter 19. The final chapter of the book, the last part of our conversation. It's the only solution to escape the fate that lies in store for us.

CHAPTER 19

The Solution

The fate of the Republican Party is in doubt. It is now fractured between the traditional, RINO, swamp creature, never-Trumpers, and the 74 million members of Donald Trump's populist coalition. The Republican Party can no longer survive if it continues with business as usual.

So what's the solution?

Well, here's my solution. Forming a new third party isn't the answer, as Teddy Roosevelt and his Bull Moose Party found out in 1912. It just elected Democrat Woodrow Wilson. However, drastic action is still required. The choice is simple, bold, and clear—dissolve the Republican Party as we know it and form a new party. The Republican Party, as it currently exists, days are numbered anyway.

First, we have to give this new party a new name. I considered the Conservative Party, but that has negative connotations for some. Next, I considered the Populist Party, which seemed superficially appealing. But that name would be troubling for others for entirely different reasons. Then, it hit me square in the face. It has to be called "The Freedom Party."

So this new freedom party needs a new symbol as well. My first choice is the bald eagle because it soars freely through the skies. But it is already our national bird and is on the Great Seal. So my choice is the American buffalo. This noble animal roamed freely over the Great Plains of this country for centuries before being killed off by Indians and settlers alike, just as the mighty elephant symbol is currently being killed off. What would be a more fitting symbol for The Freedom Party?

Ronna McDaniel, Chair of the Republican National Committee, pay close attention. The fate and future of your party is teetering on the brink. Donald Trump's approval rating among Republicans in a Gallup poll taken ten days after the January 6, 2021, attack on the Capitol is still at 82 percent, with some polls showing an even higher percentage. What does that tell you about who holds the future of the party? The Trump coalition of 74 million needs to be held together, with or without Donald Trump at its head.

And the only way to do that is create a new party whose name symbolizes what is most important to those 74 million people—freedom.

Any Republican member of the House or Senate that voted to impeach or convict President Trump must be primaried and defeated by the new Freedom Party. The never-Trumpers and Swamp members of the Republican Party worked against Trump in both 2016 and 2020. They were never part of the Populist coalition and aren't needed or wanted in the new Freedom Party. Let them go back to the Democrats that they sided with. That leaves the most important cog in the wheel left: the 74 million people average Americans, the real populist coalition. It is they who must be held together and convinced to join the new Freedom Party because without them there is no base.

So here is my message to those 74 million. Don't you dare let the Democrats and their protectors in the media, Big Tech, Hollywood, and big business intimidate you. You are not deplorables or undesirables or racists or Nazis or white supremacists or terrorists. You are not responsible for the actions of those anarchists and criminals that stormed the Capitol on January 6. They will and should be punished, but you should not. You freely voted for your choice for president in 2020 as was your right, at least until now. You should not be threatened with being censored from social media or canceled or lose your job or fear injury or harm to yourselves or you families, or any other damage. You don't need to be reeducated or deprogrammed, as the Left is suggesting. Don't be depressed or discouraged. Don't give up hope. Don't throw up your hands, give up, and don't vote again next time because you feel that the election may have been stolen from you. This is exactly what the Democrats and the Left want you to do. It is playing right into their hands. It will just allow them to totally consolidate all power in their hands and give them total control over your lives.

What is needed now is a second American Revolution. Just so the Left is clear, this revolution will *not* be fought with guns, muskets, cannon, assault rifles, or tanks. This will be a political revolution based on words, thoughts, ideas, and principles. From this, revolution will arise a new freedom party, replacing the old worn-out swamp in both parties. This party will be built on the Populist coalition that Donald Trump formed. Its principles will be first and foremost liberty, then individual choice and responsibility, free enterprise, America First but not alone, strong borders, peace through might and a strong military, the right to bear arms, the right to life after viability, patriotism and law and order, equality under the law for all, school choice, and standing up to and curbing China.

This is what the 74 million of you must do. Start small, on the local level. Either run for your local school board yourself, or elect members who will reject the 1619 Project that pollutes the minds of our children about American history. Contact your state legislators and demand that they ensure the integrity of the mail-in ballot system, by requiring photo IDs, signature comparisons, ballots being dated and received by election day, and voter rolls being purged of dead people, and those who no longer live in the state. Vote out of office all never-Trumpers and RINO swamp Republicans.

But most importantly, be prepared to talk to your Democratic and Independent friends, who will inevitably be turned off by the radical, socialist policies of the Biden administration. It's already starting. There were 11,000 jobs lost when the Keystone XL Pipeline ended. The assault on coal, oil, and natural gas will be swift and costly. The resulting job loss and devastation to the economy will reverberate through countless states. People will need somewhere to turn as the country is sacrificed on the altar of climate change and open borders and sanctuary cities and higher taxes and America last and gun confiscation and late-term abortions up to the very moment of birth and lockdowns and government control of all aspects of life and suppression of free speech and termination of private health insurance and elimination of school choice and the ultimately one-party totalitarianism. Welcome all those disenchanted moderates with open arms into the Freedom Party.

There are two final thoughts that come to mind. The first is Patrick Henry's famous quote, "Give me liberty or give me death." Those simple but powerful words, drive home that freedom is worth fighting for and dying for. Think of how many brave men and women have given their lives for our freedom. They did it, so we could be free to speak our minds, to vote for whom we choose, and to write books like this. They must be rolling over in their graves watching the censorship and cancel culture running wild in the country today.

I will end on this note. Remember the final scene in the Mel Gibson's Best Picture winner, *Braveheart*. When William Wallace was about to be beheaded on the guillotine, he was asked to renounce his rebellion against the British tyranny. The executioner said that the prisoner wished to speak. What word did William Wallace scream out as loudly as he could? *Freedom!* That's the same word that everyone that still loves this country should be screaming at the top of his or her lungs—Freedom! Freedom! Freedom! Without our precious freedom, the United States of America is no more. And that, my friends, is unacceptable to me. What say you?

I say:

About the Author

Gil Grossi has been on the inside of the political and legal world his whole professional career. After getting his degree in political science from the University of Illinois, he worked as a Cook County prosecutor for eleven years. Gil then became a judge, where he spent twenty-three years in the Cook County Court system. While on the bench, he also taught law at night for twenty-three years. Gil has additionally done work as an arbitrator, mediator, adoption guardian, and election hearing officer. Now in semi-retirement, he is still in the arena as an administrative law judge for a Chicago area suburban village.

Gil lives in the western suburbs of Chicago with his wife, sons, and dog, Cody. He just became a grandfather for the first time. Gil is a trivia fanatic, playing competitively for nearly twenty years. He has written a soon-to-be-published trivia book as well.

www.ingramcontent.com/pod-product-compliance
Lightning Source LLC
Chambersburg PA
CBHW031148250726
48655CB00002B/888